A Gathering Sense *of* Light

Maggie Slattery

A Gathering Sense *of* Light

Acknowledgements

There are many. To all who have accompanied me at different times,
I extend my deepest thanks.

I wish to thank my family, especially John, for enriching me with
time, space, and encouragement; Kelé and Simone, for understanding
my need to write about them; Jude Aquilina, my inspirational poetry
teacher and mentor; Kate Cullity, sister-friend, who frequents my
red couch and enthusiastically reads my work; Anni Sutton, my great
friend and attentive muse; and my sisters, brothers, late parents and
grandfather, with whom I have much in common.

To John, who understands light

A Gathering Sense of Light
ISBN 978 1 76041 324 8
Copyright © text Maggie Slattery 2017
Cover image © Yann Forget/Wikimedia Commons/CC-BY-SA-3.0

First published 2017 by
GINNINDERRA PRESS
PO Box 3461 Port Adelaide 5015 Australia
www.ginninderrapress.com.au

Contents

Foreword	7
Just another day	9
Grandfather	10
Climbing Yosemite's Half Dome	11
Coming Home	12
Separation	13
Convergence	14
Lorikeets	16
Hymn for S	17
Late afternoon bushwalk	18
Pan Pipes	19
After Here	20
Lullaby	22
High Summer	23
The Reverend	24
Remembering Him	25
Returning	26
Prelude Sonnet	27
all power and glory	28
I Promise You	30
The Curdimurka Ball	31
Cherry Earrings	32
Where she goes	33
Flight	34
Dark Heart	35
Donald	36
Tim of the Lane	37
Colebrook	38
Four Snapshots	39
Unbounded	43

Puddles	45
Ethel Dread, 1965	46
Trying to See	47
Three Sisters	49
Aaron's Light	50
Boy	51
Jumping Rope	55
Bicycle Accident	56
Yellow Kite	57

Foreword

In the living room of my childhood home, three small bookshelves boasted the neat volumes of *Encyclopedia Britannica* that conceived my love for anatomical drawings, layered transparencies and interleaved tissue paper.

When I was ten years old, an illustrated edition of Dante's *Divine Comedy*, given to my unsuspecting parents, appeared on the bottom shelf – and I disappeared (with it), behind the couch, into the light between shadows. A promise, born then, returns again from exile in the form of this collection of poems written during the past two years since my sixtieth birthday.

The poems reflect returning patterns of descent and ascent during decades of my life, through memories whose arrows have the sharpest tips. Each attempts to bring its subject into equal light. Some follow strict form; others have found their own shape; all exist for a reason. They are released into their readers' worlds, perhaps to rest on the bottom shelf of a corner library… or to disappear, like the copy of Dante's *Divine Comedy* lost in the hellfire of the backyard incinerator after I was discovered examining the illustrated engraving of Gustave Doré's *Arachne in Purgatory*. They endure, nonetheless, as my liberators.

> Differing voices join to sound sweet music;
> so do the different orders on our life
> render sweet harmony among these spheres.
> Dante, Par. 6 124–26

Just another day

Blue dissolves
and brooding thoughts
gather like seagulls
sorting through matter
caught up in the froth
of the hours rolled past.

I'm never ready
when you come, never
ready to leave you.

Grandfather

On a day like this – southerly
blowing a gale, the sea a smelly
blue paddock of frothing cauliflowers
– grandfather took to the beach

where boys criss-crossed the sand
carrying wet bucketloads for men
who formed the bulging mounds
into dragons, knights and castles.

We leaned over the jetty railings
above creaking, wave-slapped, elephant
leg piers. White-green seawater growled
through the slippery, splintered boards.

On a day like this, I turned into a hooked
fish, flung into the air, flailing at the edge
of its tether, stung by terror equal to god's
stark, cold, everywhereness.

I wanted my grandfather's giant hands
to scoop me up into his thick net of wet wool,
feel the relief of his stubbled chin against
the white scales of my bloodless face.

Climbing Yosemite's Half Dome

Sheer tectonic beauty, metamorphosed ash,
granite bosomed coronet in a meadow bed.

Your feet dance with suitors, lured by your crown,
seekers of solace, monkey mad and peak obsessed.

You know him well, this man approaching,
who announces himself dome-worthy.

You indulge his fancies. He strokes his thanks:
a climbing poet, plotting to publish your blush.

But you inscribe the scribe, this cocked wordsmith,
leaping to conclusion, almost at his peak.

You cut him short, your prized summit in his view,
and dangle him blizzard-whipped in his flimsy tent.

You send his white-out mind away to face you;
near freeze his body in its nylon cocoon.

He hangs, silenced by your might,
crestfallen, his tumbled tome lying at your feet.

Coming Home

for K

Twilight scarcely glints on the orange girders
of Golden Gate Bridge, above the thick, late afternoon fog
that reconfigures the seasons. We're southbound,
heading home into the wintry summer mist that swallows
pastel-bright houses. Cyprus trees in Golden Gate Park
reach out with eerie limbs. Strange dark blue-green
eucalypts huddle in tall, shy packs, oily and inelegant.
I know them another way – in their own land,
where they play with the wind in a wide blue sky.
Here they wax and thrust from rich, wet soil,
fighting to claim the overcrowded light.
We reach Potrero Hill, car-drugged, as yellow rays
flute over the vapour petticoats of Twin Peaks.
It will soon be night, though starry light is fogged.
I dream we are still coming home,
through ghostly trees standing wide apart.
I am fighting against a clouded membrane
to reclaim the golden hue that coloured our day
while you, imbued with incorruptible light,
walk through your country of beauty and drought.

Separation

Decisions hard made
fall from chaos into
imperfect results;
never-endings tied
to unseen beginnings.
There is no Gordian cut –
yes from no; no from yes.
Either way, between new
formations, constellations
fracture, pieces break
apart, like chunks
of planet sent into orbit
by a colliding asteroid.
A direction of itself decrees.
The cost is eternal, everyone
pays, no winner takes all,
and each must realign,
like newfound words
stumbling into an open verse.

Convergence

for J

Yesterdays settle,
perfect coals
of red white light
fading to grey.

After all, our children,
new exquisite flames,
reveal our imprinted
stories

circling again and again
carrying us
back to the river.

We try to disentangle
from our abstractions
lapping
at its edge,
unattended,
like forgotten tinnies
clanking, sinking

into quiet
now
that draws us in
from our perceiving
circumference
to the mirrored sun,
reflecting
across the water.

Stay close, my friend.
I am deep in
and your symmetry
is my boat.

Lorikeets

Sling shot
flashes of green and yellow
piercing the air

love-flung
quivers of creation,
impossible to halt.

I've seen you suspended
mid-air, bodies upright,
tails holding anchor,

wings beating furiously
in a hummingbird moment,

soundless in the effort
to be still.

I try to meditate, hold back
those incessant
words of prey.

It is not a quiet activity –
thoughts flying, immutable.

Hymn for S

Sing, as if all of life listens,
as I once heard your earliest, single
tone that sustained gestation's
first refrain, singing time
into our unity.

I realise, through you,
that listening is belonging,
and I am transposed as
your sound traces unexpected
outlines of splendour.

I hear you sing into the day
in the sudden melodies flying
from the canopies of tall,
still trees, returning our
song, revivified.

Your voice opens into
the enclosures of night's cathedral,
dispels the whisperings of empty
rooms, bundles ordinary life
into unforeseen gifts.

Leave no note unvisited.
Transcend disequilibrium.
Restore the sustaining truth
of our earliest songs.
Sing into your life, always.

Late afternoon bushwalk

At the bushland edge, bull ants
loop with percussive haste, spiralling
about like the mind's ruminations.
The elements sound in magpie warblings,
corella rucking, doves' kookawook,
and a hush that swells between sounds –
that sudden stillness wrapped in the distant
rumble of traffic, the timid, faltering first note
of a kookaburra, a far away crow, an overhead
plane. Someone calls for their dog; a tennis
racket thwops; insects rise in a cloud
from the grass and the concert continues
till long night shadows swallow the day.

Pan Pipes

for Jude

Water-laden
reed capillaries,
one upon the other,
merry go round
love me not
melodies, borne
of Syrinx transformed,
escaping from Pan
who spoke of love
on the river's edge,
(poor sod),
his trembling mouth
on the hollowed nymph
plucked from the River Laden.

After Here

for Kate

I am the man,
        underneath the sky   exposed
                                                                   out of the blue
lost
        husband,
        father,
        friend, brother, son
torn
        from an ordinary day.   I am
affections sustained by memory;

                                                 the disappearance
of patterned days,
        stories carried home
        at night.

I am   my beloved's tears,
                  the thin, dry sound
from her throat;   the gate
that never opens;   traces
of footsteps; my smell
in our unmade bed;   clothes
left empty.   I am
                                            the bottom of
                                            too many bottles

of red wine;
posthumous awards;   life
insurance;
diary entries;   the same
                                            silent
                                            face

in photographs.

I was   all I could have been,
I am   all   my
               loved ones   will become.

Lullaby

In my papery age, hardened
by fifty Australian summers,
I remember my youth's silken fabric
patterned with opening buds catching
light. Raven hair, paisley pinks,
orange plumpness; sun-dazed reds.
Looking back, I see it all in motion,
rocking, passing through interludes –
new motifs forming around the old;
words sung at the breast, disappearing
and returning newborn into another
epoch, freshly remembered and reformed
from melodies as ancient as the stars.
I cannot conceive of a greater song.

High Summer

Heat arrives on white hot currents
that push old dogs into the shade
of the stippled jacaranda canopy
where magpies scratch in vain.
In these hottest hours I wonder
why I live in this cruel place that only
German tourists could love. The smooth
gold of their youthful skin mocks me,
a wilted bloom, declaiming the misfortune
of my freckled forebears who were plunged
into this searing, crackling southern fire
to escape the empty potato pot. I look
for solace in my over-stuffed furniture,
sitting swollen in the strangled dark.
Across the veranda, coming into view,
a gleaming ephemeral jewel hovers
above the horizon of my sunburnt yard.
Everything is penetrated by a deep stillness,
silencing even the crows. Muffled sounds
spread like a pulse that distills each
suspended moment to a quality of pure
hypnotic waiting. My body eases in response.
I am not discontent, sensing now the barely
perceptible changes of light and air movement,
the tendrils of a twilight breeze that reach
into the heat, slowly perforating its parched,
heavy curtain. When the longed-for sound
of car tyres crunches over gravel,
and wagging tails stir dust into the air, I jump
to my feet, setting the dogs to dancing
another summer evening round.

The Reverend

A long, black, vertical line
shimmered in the distance.

It grew taller with each stride,
bringing into detail Father Farrell's
ankle-length cassock.

(How long did it take him to negotiate
the score of tiny cloth covered buttons?)

The effect of wind and the flick of his chin
tousled his shoulder-length auburn hair.

Perhaps a sermon was forming inside his head,
or a recipe, an art critique, a Latin translation?

He charged daily through the school yard, like
a tornado of tormented energy gouging its path

from another world: of theatre, art, music,
exotic food, native gardens, travellers' tales.

His housing trust home was an ark of gifted paintings,
his muses drawn to him – Bonython, Preston, O'Toole,
Helpmann – and my mother.

He was the lighthouse in my childhood sea; yet
a shipwreck in the eyes of his parishioners.

My mother, his bookkeeper, knew
the immeasurable gift of philosophical friendship.

By his account, she saw where life and imagination
meet, and in his garden found nature restored.

Remembering Him

The bone-thin man squats, elbow on one knee,
slouch hat tipped back from his brow, like a bloke.
He squints, as if subjected to overwhelming light.
The sepia jungle behind him seems bland, empty.

> 'It's not what it looks like.'
> He finally says something, forty years later.
> 'There were bodies, everywhere.'
> Two sentences. No more.

The thin man squats, elbow leaning on one knee,
in front of a bare, wooden house propped on stumps.
He's not smiling. Nor is baby four (of seven),
propped awkwardly against his left shoulder.

The man, thicker now, leans his elbows on the kitchen
table. His palms are pressed against his eyes.
He's crying, listening to the Anzac march broadcast.
Outside, his children play with his war medals.

He's not yet sixty when his marching orders
come again. His hair is grey, his body swollen.
Mostly, he sits outside, elbows on knees,
listening to the birds, sipping tea, drinking beer.

He wants to die, he says (but he is terrified).
The jungle is closing in and he does not escape.
It took him without mercy, like all the rest.
You could see it coming, in his eyes.

Returning

I look to you for misplaced fragments,
knowing it's not the past we crave
but the joining conversation
of our familiar exchange.

We try to remember each other
as now pretends the present
under thick and covering layers
that barely represent us.

We compose ourselves in stories
that stir the dust, picking up,
week by week, the wakening echoes
roused by the truth between our words.

In the telling and the laughing,
we dance around the silent space
of unconfronted hesitations to touch
the spark that brought us here.

Prelude Sonnet

Scented corollas of petals unfold
like silken pinwheels, tiny spring banners
fluttering in the pollinating wind
to herald Persephone's arrival.
She ascends swiftly through the sweetened sap,
released from her underground winter world.
Hades, forsaken, flings a gossamer net
of snow, on blossoms, charming her return
to his kingdom beneath the waking world.
She gestures warmth toward the fragile ice
and strides, emboldened by the dawning light,
past the first grasshopper, to greet the sun.
Bees chorus nature's purpose, pollen stirred,
and she, with her opening song, concurs.

all power and glory

(oh lord, not to you!)

his holiness is ringing in
new bishops inside
the vatican basilica
with vested men
lining the pews
while outside in the square
patient tourists watch
delta headdresses
bobbing and bowing
on screen

then the doors open
spewing forth a few
lowly nuns followed by
a scattering of monks
bespectacled seminarians
ordinary priests
newly greened
and plain old bishops
and finally
the unrepentant
cardinals
laced up
with colour-coded
glory
all the way
to the top
of purple

his holiness leaves
white
through the back door.

I Promise You

I wait, to move toward you,
like light below a microscope slide.
Do you approach?
Meet me with your eye,
between our converging worlds.
Are you looking?
Lift the stage to reveal my whereabouts.
Can you see?
The coarsest lens will tell you
where I am.
I'm too easily lost
under higher magnification.
Find me first,
many times over,
that our startled souls
might know
of other spheres.

The Curdimurka Ball

Yellow moonlight seeps through a sand
cloud, near the endless pink-white crust
of Lake Kati Thanda. A tarpaulin ballroom
strains on its moorings. Primped hairdos
inflate like dry steelo pads, trousered
thighs are cling-wrapped, and punters
move about, hunched over like amateur
actors in a geriatric comedy.

The restaurant tent is imitating a bloated
marshmallow. Waiters fight with white linen
table tops ajangle with percussive cutlery
out of sync with a stage band competing
with the wind. Stalwart couples, dancing
on a lean, are bulging galleons swaying back
and forth, unnoticed by batches of red-faced
bachelors who raise shouts of beers to the odds
of drowning without water.

When the sun rises through a sandpapered sky,
all is still. The dance floor is empty. Crusted eyes
are clogged with sand; tents lie dishevelled.
The inflated memory of a long-gone railway
is upheld, yet again, at the abandoned Curdimurka
siding – by eight hundred paying guests
and a willy-willy dust devil.

Cherry Earrings

It rattled into the street
behind the old gelding –
a cartload of dismal harvest:
winter greens lined up
like drab veterans
of a post-war world weighed
down by the pound, hungry
children and scant shillings
scraped from a kitchen jar.

The end of bleakness
was heralded by an epiphany
of cherries – radiant markers
on the ecliptic; sumptuous
jewels for the deaf ears
of baby boomers cartwheeling
into the future.

Where she goes

When the wind strips
her songbirds' branches,
she is gone, back to the window,
high above men's swaying bodies,
dolphin wet on the grass.
They play world-ready games,
as dogs bark indifference
to her Rapunzel state.
Fortune tilts her.
She watches their bellies laughing,
hears the spluttering
of her words, flying blind
into the blue splintering sky.
They tease and turn,
and she is falling – into
the apathetic streets, wheeling
amongst people going the other way.
She feels the strike of pavement,
draws breath, breath, breath,
proclaims the consequential
child of her perverted fate.

Waiting to alight,
her songbirds fly
against the resounding wind
that augurs her mad.

Flight

A distraction of chirps
broadcasts from a nest
in the lilly pilly tree.
I listen…
to a call, rising
from my solar plexus,
beckoning me out
of my casing,
away from the shape
of impressions
I try so hard to maintain,
as if I will die if uncovered.

Staying on the precipice
at the edge of the nest
is death. The honeyeater
sings a lifeline
for its fledglings
to fly up quickly
from their discarded shells,
not thinking
of the ground.

Everything broken open
is mirrored in the sky today
where honeyeaters
are beginning again
to fly.

Dark Heart

Exhibition, Art Gallery of South Australia, March 2014

Menace draws the eye
to a trapped spider,
fighting for time,
as cuckoos call out of sync
through hollow skull sockets, too late
to warn the dead.

Delicate flowers fade
in the shadow of corporate logos, ghoulish
in the screen-lit glow of violent clashes.
War plays on, as poets
rhyme of god, miracles,
songs and streams.

Life is flamed
in the play of darkness, tempting
hearts to open bare
beneath the spears
descending from ancestors, daring
all to know the crossing.

Petrified life vests
catch a shoreless wave
and there is no escape,
only respite, in the café
spruiking light refreshments
between the darkness
and the day.

Donald

His dark brown eyes blinked clueless
in the sheepish quiet that followed
simple questions. Any calculation
was unfathomable to his brain.
Facts slipped, like the glossy
cap of his thick black hair,
over his head, toward
an unintelligible
vanishing
point.

His brother, constant, beside him, could
spell, recite times tables, remember
the date, speak on his behalf,
with shared knowledge
of two brains as one,
the intimate sum
of duet parts;
until…

'For the best,' a Special School bus
began to arrive at their house each day.
No one could stop the driver from taking
Donald – day after day, in the shed,
unmonitored, unknown, with
a subtracting intimacy
secured by silence
and the power
to take one
away
from
one.

Tim of the Lane

Tim's chair is
a white plastic
finders keepers throne
that sits in the lane
overlooking a swale

Tim's bed is
a grimy starlit
finders keepers swag
on a patch of the lane
hidden from view

Tim's day is
a take away
finders keepers coffee
and afternoon chips
with a can of beer

Tim's life is
a shortened
finders keepers straw
fallen into decay
before its time.

Colebrook*

1960

We are standing by a fence,
close enough to touch.
Our worlds are divided
by wire diamonds.
Behind you, children sit still,
on a bare veranda, watching.
On my side, noisy kids run
merry-go-round between
swings and see-saws.
My mother is unpacking a picnic.
A bell rings and you are gone.

---

* Colebrook Home, now Colebrook Reconciliation Park

Four Snapshots

K with teddy bear
Haight Ashbury Nursery School 1983

Four ducklings make their way across
the front of your San Francisco sweatshirt.
Your hands are in view, long fingers
waiting inside of dimpled flesh.

Your tricycle is on the path
as you pause for the photographer,
Casey Jones cap turned backwards,
pouting lips smeared with jam.

Bangs of blonde hair fall from your crown,
feathering your brow, above piercing eyes.
Teddy is looking out from his snug,
peering one-eyed over your collar.

S at two and a quarter
Adelaide 1990

You sit on a kiddy chair
underneath a crepe myrtle tree.

Its show of papery red blossoms
highlights your rosiness.
The yard is bare, except for you
and the cast of your imagination.

You hold a golden toy umbrella
above your tamed curls.

A perimeter of lipstick wobbles
around your rosebud mouth

pursed for the camera.

Great Uncle John

His eyes
are jelly wrapped
chocolate drops
with soft centres.

His mouth
a wide semicircle
that joins his eyebrows
whenever he sees you.

His Adam's apple
leaps about,
declaring
his delight.

K with piercings
Adelaide, 2002

Above your smiling eyes,
proud, angry flesh announces
your latest piercing.

Black-lined lips
match the long hair that borders
your pancaked face.

Flip side of the jagged
cardboard picture frame
you make a wish:

Happy Birthday Mum,
love K.

Unbounded

>The astronaut drifts, momentarily
>free of instructions, like an infant
>looking out from its mother's lap,
>joined with the tempo of all things
>spiralling in space at the same speed.

Inside the alien anvil-pounding MRI capsule,
her future hammers into focus. She is enveloped
by overpowering whiteness. Tubes wind
across the hospital floor, up walls, through ceilings,
wrapping the building with their coiling briars.

>No fear divides her here.
>Gravity has no pull.
>Her visored suit
>reflects light into the vastness;
>she is not insignificant.

A timpani belts out her diagnosis. Dark clouds
amass on the lighted glass. Time changes shape.

>All attention is gathered for each task,
>until preparations for re-entry are complete.
>She knows the volatile partnering
>of propulsion and explosion.

Her tunnelled senses are strangely suspended.
She remembers the rich smell of life –
fodder and waste; strangers and friends; dirt
and disappointment. She aches with care.

In her season of fire, as bursting pods explode,
she is gathered into the tempo
of all things, spiralling in space
at the same speed.

Puddles

In liquid state suspended briefly,
thin rimmed equilibrium,
viscous, spreading,
contracting, pulsing,
barely held edges
surrendering:
boundless,
transitioned;
earth quenched,
birds flown,
boots drenched.

Ethel Dread, 1965

Scrawny bloodhound; accursed misery-maker
of grade seven girls: we, all breast buttons, downy
mounds, moist secrets – her guilty prisoners,
doing hard labour.
There was no breaking away, no pushing
against the cane.
We could only graduate.

Trying to See

The hilltop church
looks over Fremantle
Harbour and Rottnest Island.

She says he would
have liked the outlook.

His infant son stares
at the motorcycle helmet
perched on the narrow,
lacquered lid, amongst
lilies and roses.

An old man drones
in heartfelt verse.
He's one foot in the grave,
half an ear gone,
eyes deeply soft
from a lifetime of seeing pain.

He promises to make sense of this
in forgotten allegory.

In the end,
comfort is taken
by the dead, in repose,
where sins are forgiven,
or at least amended.

Torment stays behind,
and hope is shifted
to the shoulders of children,
turning to follow
the wooden box,
toward the view.

Three Sisters

We lie on the grass,
shrouded by the fabric of night,
in liminal space suspended by heat
falling mercurial away from the sun.

Three skinny silhouettes,
dancing limbs entwined,
reach toward the Southern Cross,
diamonds on our fingertips.

We are lunatic kids – moonstruck
make-believers, wild with sugars
of apricots and red-skinned plums;
freckled from sandy beaches.

Our luminous playhouse
is charged with giggle,
leaf crackle and birdcall –
night airs played on timeless lutes.

We thrill endless space with bold
ideas and fierce intent, pleasure
flowing through our pert silliness,
into everything existing.

Aaron's Light

Your eyes open after little sleep. It's him.
He woke you again and again through the night.
Dreams move in fragments, just out of reach,
like the mobile dangling above his cot.

Tomorrow, you will touch his perfect body,
love his shape and breadth, his spiky hair.
He is the river flowing fast from its origins,
a force always greater than you, never yours.

Your feet are sinking into riverbank mud.
You have never wandered; you don't know how
to leave the shore. He is your charge, your son,
born to become light's miraculous blossoming.

You are not imagining. Toys line the walls
of his room. Which house was that? His tricycle
is red. He is riding, cheeky grin, full of life. He is
right here, a man, and you are standing on the bank.

He will stay thirty-six. You will grow old, wishing
he would wake you again.

Boy

I

Your name stays inside the mouth
of angels who want you back.

On earth, where you reside,
they make a foil for remembering.

People forget you're here,
cannot pronounce you.

Your name sticks in their throat,
never rolling across the tongue,

to sound you on a feather,
give breath to your life.

Some say you never arrived.

Born soundless, blue.
No one breathing.

II

Your lower half is waterweed,
still swimming in between
the currents, bound slowly
shoreward, yet to plunge,
wave-tossed, into life.

Your upper half is blue lit,
tied to a balloon that floats up
for a kestrel's view, rising
into light bouncing back
through sapphire eyes.

In between, vertebrae snake
like an unearthed power line
too soon to straighten. So you
use your hands and knees,
create a bridge to the earth.

Like Atlas, you carry for all
a load too big to pass along.
If you let go, earth will fall.
But humankind, clueless,
only sees you failing.

Your spine lengthens under
the weight of your mind deepening.
Unnoticed, with head bowed,
your feet learn the earth,
then push into flight.

III

The boy kept a chrysalis
in a jar on the kitchen shelf.
He made drawings of butterflies
and pinned them on the wall.

At just the right moment
the insect emerged, paused
to dry its wings, and waited
for the lid to open.

Then the boy covered himself
in a fine membrane, wound
round his body so that his arms
were pinned against his sides.

Inside his cocoon, he dreamed
of flying, to his father,
wearing magic sunglasses
with superhero powers.

A moment too soon,
he emerged, paused, and fell
into a spider's web,
spellbound by the night.

He dyed his wings black,
pierced holes in his skin,
and flew against the glass,
as if the lid might open.

IV

In praise of Epimetheus

Zeus, praise the unsung man
who sees, through reflection,
forces colliding in momentum's wake,
the rollout of human haste.
His Titan twin stole fire,
and though you chained him,
already the lanyard was pulled,
firing flames of foresight
into the breeched bellies
of mortal men. In the shadow
of spent life, with hindsight
lighting another way,
this man is formed
of a slower, thoughtful body.
Animals draw near him,
breathe in his regard.

His voice circles the planet,
articulating hope.
Praise the young man, Zeus,
unavowed in you.

Jumping Rope

Turners chant,
drum the ground,
pulse the air, beckoning.

Skippers wait,
at the funnel's edge, every
cell whirring like propellers
ready for takeoff.

Figures of eight flying under,
over, spiralling around
slipstreams, rhythms
rhyming, counting

one, two,
another through,
three, me, connecting
you, wheeling, looping,

drooping, reeling,
braids swinging
body stitched
beat skipped

foot tripped
rope flipped
over.
Out!

Bicycle Accident

metal, motion, body, thoughts
cruising down a steep course
in early daylight
childlike
sweet
                       turning
bitter
dream like
in eerie blue light
through the intersection
sirens, body, metal, motion

Yellow Kite

The
kite leaps
from my grasp
like a bird of paradise
dancing upward with its long tail
trailing underneath; unaware of its maker
and its reliance on the person holding on to the line
of connection between earth and sky, faithfully distributing
the tension of flight, answering each tug and dip as the
yellow diamond of bright plastic receives the
wind. At its upmost point, limited only
by the length of a borrowed orange
ball of yarn, it moves through
side to side and looping
spiral patterns like a
Balinese dancer
of surreal
grace
;
o
n
;
a
n
d

o
n
;
a
n
d

o
n
;

www.ingramcontent.com/pod-product-compliance
Lightning Source LLC
Chambersburg PA
CBHW062203100526
44589CB00014B/1930